The Happy Winter Guide

Use 7 Hygge Strategies & Your Happiness Superpower to Defeat Winter Blues

Copyright © Jeanine Byers

December 2017

All rights reserved.

The unauthorized reproduction or distribution of this copyrighted work is illegal. Criminal copyright infringement, including infringement without monetary gain, is investigated by the FBI and is punishable by up to 5 years in federal prison and a fine of $250,000.

This book is dedicated to all of my readers who suffer from winter blues each year. May you find the solutions you need and experience the delight of summer in each dark, cold day of winter.

The Questions

Do You Have Winter Blues?

Which are Your Most Difficult Symptoms?

How Can the Magic of Hygge Help You with Winter Blues?

How Can You Make Light Therapy Your Biggest Resource?

How about a Morning Shot of Sunlight?

Would Waking Up with a Dawn Simulator Help?

What Might Change for You if You Used a Light Box Every Day?

Which Kind of Exercise Could You Befriend this Winter?

Would Rebounding Be Fun for You?

What about Dancing?

Do You Enjoy Walking?

What about Low Impact Aerobics?

What if You Created a Space All Your Own? A Hygge Comfort Nook

How Might Adding Texture & Softness Comfort You?

Would Vitamin D Help?

What about Boosting Serotonin with Carbohydrates?

How Might You Create Special Moments with the Ones You Love Most this Winter?

How Will You Use this Information to Transform Your Winter Experience?

The Happy Winter Guide Web Pages

Do You Know These 5 Facts about the Author?

These are the questions. Read on to discover & personalize the answers…

Do You Have Winter Blues?

"Life naturally slows down in winter. The days grow shorter, light becomes scarce, and we respond by planting ourselves in front of the television or hiding under the covers to stay warm. But how do you know when a seasonal slump is a more serious problem?" - Psycom.net

I think it was one of my roommates who told me about seasonal affective disorder. She'd read an article describing it and thought it might be the reason I was depressed.

I was in my 20s at the time, and had never heard of it. By the time I finished reading the article, I knew that was exactly what was wrong, and was so relieved to have an explanation.

In the many years that followed, I tried a lot of things that didn't help.

With hygge, I have been reminded of a few things that did and found others that I hadn't heard or thought of before.

"The reduced light, warmth, and color of winter can leave you feeling melancholy, irritable, or tired. But if these feelings recur each year, make it tough to function during the winter months, and then subside in spring or early summer, you may be suffering from seasonal affective disorder (SAD)." HelpGuide.com

People often use the terms "winter blues" and "seasonal affective disorder" interchangeably, because both occur as a result of the lessening sunlight available that occurs as fall becomes winter and both make winter difficult for a lot of people who don't live near the equator or in places where the seasons don't change at all.

But the latter is an official diagnostic term for people who have symptoms of Major Depression during the winter. The former can include a few of the symptoms, some of them, most or all, but is a term for those who haven't been diagnosed.

Many people experience the symptoms without being diagnosed and may go through several difficult winters before getting an official diagnosis. Others are never diagnosed and do their best to cope with symptoms on their own.

For the most part, I will use the term winter blues in this book, but keep in mind that if you do have a diagnosis of seasonal affective disorder, and are working with a therapist, this book is only meant to augment the help you receive in therapy, not to replace it.

And here's the question I want you to take with you as you read this book…

How can I use what I am reading, in my own life, so that each winter is better than the last one?

I will ask you questions at the end of each section that will help you answer that question and personalize the information for yourself. Doing so can help you craft a powerful plan for lessening the impact of winter blues.

But after you've read the book, if you need any help putting together your winter blues plan, and would like to talk it through in a coaching session with me, go to

comfortwithhygge.com/herosjourneycoaching

Which are Your Most Difficult Winter Blues Symptoms?

"The most commonly reported SAD symptoms include significant fatigue, pervasively sad mood, loss of interest in activities, sleeping more than usual, craving and eating more starches and sweets, gaining at least 5 percent of body weight and difficulty concentrating." -APA.org

Winter blues makes life's demands more difficult to do. The symptoms each person have indicate the way it shows up for them and the severity of symptoms determine just how difficult it is each winter.

(1) Having less energy or motivation for the normal things you do every day

(2) Craving carbohydrates and sweets & overeating so that weight gain is possible

(3) Wanting to sleep more than usual or having difficulty getting up in the mornings or insomnia (or both)

(4) Feelings of irritability

(5) Feelings of depression or sadness, not enjoying the things you normally like to do

(6) Finding it difficult to concentrate on things, brain fog or foggy thinking

Winter blues, or seasonal affective disorder, is caused by less available sunlight and it has many, if not most or all, of the symptoms of depression. But with SAD, the symptoms occur in fall and winter and go away when full sunlight returns.

Personalizing this Section

Do you recognize your own winter experience in any of the descriptions presented?

Which symptoms do you usually experience during winter?

Which ones are the most difficult for you?

How Can the Magic of Hygge Help You with Winter Blues?

"Hygge is the light in the darkness, which carries us through six cold winter months, and it has done so for more than a thousand years." -Marie Tourell Soderbcrg

Hygge is a word which has no easy translation into English. It seems to hold the concept of several English words combined. Peaceful cozy comfort and pleasure.

Putting your feet up while a fire blazes, and you are wrapped up in your favorite blanket or wearing your most comfortable robe. Having a great book to read and a cup of hot chocolate nearby.

Being with your family or friends and being completely comfortable as yourself, knowing you are well-loved and are about to have a great time with the people who mean the most to you.

Hygge is about an atmosphere & an experience. A feeling of home. A feeling that we are safe, that we are shielded from the world & can let our guard down."

-The Little Book of Hygge, Meik Wiking

How can hygge help you with winter blues?

Let's take a look at how Danish people handle their winters in Denmark.

They have been ranked the happiest people in the world many times in spite of very cold, very dark winters. So, I believe that we can learn a lot from the way they hygge winter about the changes we need to make our own lives happier.

From what you have read, so far, does hygge appeal to you?

Read on for hygge strategies you can try.

How Can You Make Light Therapy Your Biggest Resource?

"Regardless of what causes winter depression, bright light—particularly when delivered in the early morning—seems to reverse the symptoms."

-TheAtlantic.com

"Light therapy involves sitting in front of a light box for a certain length of time each day. It is designed to mimic bright, outdoor summer light and cause a biochemical change in the brain to lift mood and relieve symptoms of SAD."

-Minnesota State University

Quite a bit about winter blues & seasonal affective disorder is still a mystery. But they do seem to know that bright light helps, as does sunlight.

So, it is the most important strategy you can add for lessening or eliminating your winter blues symptoms.

Everything I read suggests that morning light is best of all. And that may be the difficult part for those of us who are night owls.

Not only might you have a tendency to sleep in and stay up late, but as you lose the sunlight you need, you may find it messes up your body's circadian rhythm, which could lead to staying up even later and sleeping in longer than you normally do.

You may not want to hear that early morning light is your best weapon against winter blues, and believe me, I understand. Night owl, here.

But the goal of light therapy is to make your body think it's still summer. And morning like seems to be the best way to do it.

In Denmark, Danes experience dark days for a long part of the year. Their hygge strategies involve embracing light therapy all day long.

They surround themselves with light, using candles, soft lamps that provide gentle light in their reading nooks, fireplaces cast a soft glow, and they continue living in the light all day long.

How about a Morning Shot of Sunlight?

Grab a cup of tea and a book and plant yourself outside in sunlight or inside next to a big window in a well-lit room. Cozy it up & turn it into a hygge moment.

If you can add a 15-20 minute morning walk in the sun, even better.

Would Waking Up with a Dawn Simulator Help?

One of the symptoms people often experience as a result of winter blues is difficulty getting up in the morning. One solution is to try a dawn simulator. It works while you are asleep, and what could be better than that?

A dawn simulator creates dawn by gradually brightening a light until it is at complete full spectrum brightness.

I used one myself many years ago when I worked as an addictions therapist and had to get up early each morning and it worked very well.

Not only did I wake up easily, but I felt energetic enough to get ready quickly and easily when usually, getting up in the morning meant I was sluggish & lethargic.

For me, it didn't seem to matter what time I got up, because often, the sun itself was up already. I used a floor lamp right next to where my head was and it was timed to gradually brighten over a four-hour period.

What Could Change for You if You Used a Light Box Every Day?

You may find that owning a light box and using it every day will be your best help with winter blues.

If you can create a morning routine that starts earlier, but floods you with light, that will make it easier to get ready.

Let the young ones sleep while you head for your comfort nook, turn on cozy, soft lighting around you, place your light box in front of you, and light a candle nearby. Add a hot cup of tea you can sip and savor.

I remember going on a trip to San Diego one February and on the last day I was there, I sat on the beach, on a very big rock, soaking up the sun for 3 hours. At the end of that time, I felt like it was summer.

If I could do that every day, I doubt I'd experience winter the way I do now, the way so many of us do. Light boxes seem like a good substitute for hours in the sun.

Personalizing this Section

Of these forms of light therapy, which do you think would be most powerful for you?

Would it be good to try more than one?

How would they fit into your schedule?

How to Make Each Moment Hygge

Step outside into the sunlight carrying a big cup of hot chocolate or your favorite hot tea.

Read a book while sitting in front of the light box. Light a candle, too, and drink your tea.

What are other ways you could add comfort?

Which Kind of Exercise Could You Befriend this Winter?

> *"Signe Johansen's new book How To Hygge hails the Nordic people's love of being in nature as the key to hygge, stating that 'the outdoors is preferable to the gym every time'. This is backed up by several studies which have found that those who exercise outdoors are more likely to keep up a consistent routine."*
>
> -Sara Malm for Daily Mail UK

The best exercise plan is the one you are willing to continue to do! So be inspired by the Danes determination to get outside during the winter but if you know that will never work for you, do whatever will.

I love taking walks ... occasionally. But if the right music is playing, I'll dance every single day. So, for me, jumping on my rebounder to music I love and then, dancing for 15-20 minutes to my son's playlist is more likely to work during the winter.

What is often recommended is exercising several times a week for 30-60 minutes at a time. But do what you can. Even 15 minutes is better than none.

Read on for several exercise ideas.

Would Rebounding Be Fun for You?

> *"A trampoline workout can also strengthen your body while detoxifying the cells within it."* -Dr. Axe

This exercise involves bouncing on a mini-trampoline. Rebounding can be a great choice for anyone needing low-impact exercise. And it can feel like dancing with the right music playing.

It benefits every cell in your body, is good for the lymphatic system, can help to improve your digestion, strengthens the heart, improves your immune system's functioning and does much more.

I was told once in a lecture on health and exercise that it was the best all-around exercise you could choose because it offers so many benefits. And that it's an even better choice than jogging or running. Could it become fun for you?

What about Dancing?

My father died while I was in grad school, many years ago. And I was very concerned about grieving in the "right way," so I read A LOT about how do it right, LOL. And I became determined not to gain weight because of it.

So for a year, I danced and did my own version of "aerobics" to my favorite music 3-4 times a week. It worked!

Do you love to dance, too? If you do, I recommend giving it a try to see if it could work for you.

Do You Enjoy Walking?

My mother does this several days a week, but these days she walks inside the house. She walks around her house for half an hour or so at a time.

She likes it. She puts on her music loud enough to hear it wherever she goes and then she takes off.

Walking offers many benefits, including improving your mood, strengthening your muscles and your bones, helping with balance and with coordination.

Would it work for you?

What about Low Impact Aerobics?

Though I have gone to lots of classes in my day, even jazzercise, which should have been perfect but was not, I always ended up doing things which made me winded or weren't at all fun.

So I almost gave up on aerobics, altogether. And to be honest, I don't do it now that I am older. But I used to love it and it offers many benefits.

> *"It is widely accepted that aerobic exercise improves the symptoms of depression."* -everydayhealth.com

The most aerobics fun I have ever had was dancing at home to a video created by the body double for the Flashdance movie.

I loved it!

Even though it took a while to learn the steps, once I did, I actually looked forward to coming home from work to do the workout.

Would aerobics, or dance aerobics, be fun for you?

What's most important is finding something you will love doing.

And you should check in with your healthcare practitioner before trying anything new. But exercising your way through winter, in whatever way works for you, is very hygge!

And if being motivated to exercise is not easy, here's the best reason: the endorphins you experience as a result will make winter easier.

> *"Regular exercise is a powerful way to fight seasonal depression, especially if you're able to exercise outside in natural daylight. Regular exercise can boost serotonin, endorphins, and other feel-good brain chemicals."*
>
> -HelpGuide.com

Personalizing this Section

Do you exercise regularly, and if so, does it get harder to keep going during the winter months?

Have you found a form of exercise you love?

And if not, do any of the exercise ideas above appeal to you?

Which one are you willing to try?

Making Exercise Hygge

The most important thing to do is to add music you love. Even if all you're going to do is take a quick walk.

Another possibility is to choose exercise clothing that will feel good, that make you look good, that you'll look forward to wearing while you exercise.

I also believe in rewarding yourself for taking care of yourself in this way.

I used to stop a Boston Market after going to the gym. I felt like I had earned it after going to an aerobics class and then working out with weights.

But that may not have been the healthiest reward; I'll admit it.

You could choose a new book you've wanted to read. Or a movie you have been wanting to see.

Anything that gives you warm, positive feelings as a reward for challenging yourself to take good care of yourself in this way.

How Can You Create a Space All Your Own? A Hygge Comfort Nook

Maybe you move the big comfy chair nearer to the fireplace, and create a spot for your cup of tea. Or you add a stack of textured blankets and soft throws ready to keep you warm if you need them.

Maybe you make your window seat more cozy so you can be right there when the sun comes in.

Or you cover a couch with a fuzzy warm blanket and several pillows positioned just right to watch lots of movies. Then, you clear a space on the table nearby so there will be room for everything else you need: the bowl of popcorn, the mug of hot chocolate.

What you want to do is create a comfort nook that you can go to every day that you will love, that will enfold you with warmth, and make you feel hugged or wrapped up in comfort.

I have been creating nooks like this for more than a decade, but coming to understand hygge helped me realize that they didn't always have everything I would need. Especially not for a long winter.

Light, coziness, warmth, a way to connect with the sun or with nature, a way to support moments of delight, a place to put your tea.

Take a moment to think about your home. Where would you put this nook?

I had to move things around quite a bit before I felt it had reached supreme hyggeness. But I believe that any amount of effort I or you put into creating a haven space is will be worth it.

Especially, once winter hits.

Personalizing this Section

Is there a corner or spot in your home that is oriented toward sunlight during the day, or particularly warm and cozy?

How might you make your chosen area even more cozy?

How Might Adding Texture & Softness All Comfort You this Winter?

"Decorate your home with soft textures, such as knitted or fleece throw blankets, fluffy pillows, shag rugs, & comfortable furniture. The idea here is that no matter where you sit or stand, it feels pleasant against your skin."

-Pia Edberg, The Cozy Life

One successful winter trick Danish people employ is to surround themselves with different textures as part of their comfort resources. They add blankets & pillows to couches and chairs and sometimes add plush, textured rugs.

I have tried this in my den and it really does add comfort. So, instead of decorating with a throw by tossing it artfully over the side of a couch or chair, put it on the seat, itself, so you can feel it as you lean back. Would that feel comforting?

Personalizing this Section

How could you apply this idea in every room in your home? Take a moment to scan each one mentally & jot down any ideas that come to you.

How might you use this idea in choosing what to wear each day?

Is there a way to take softness with you and have it with you wherever you go?

What will try first?

Would Vitamin D Help? Talk to Your Healthcare Provider about Vitamin D3 & Find Out if You Need More than You're Getting

"It's worth checking with your doctor to make sure your vitamin D levels are up to par. Because most U.S. adults have some type of deficiency in the vitamin, adding a supplement could help you feel better" -Dr. Axe

If you are African-American like me, or another woman of color, you are likely to have difficulty getting enough vitamin D.

But that does not mean you should just take a ton of it. I had my levels tested once and had a higher number than was recommended.

So I really want to tell anyone reading this section to check with a healthcare person you trust if you decide to try supplementing with vitamin D3.

You want be careful not to take too much. But the right amount can help if you are suffering as a result of not getting enough sunlight.

Personalizing this Section

Have you ever had your vitamin D levels checked or been told you needed to supplement with it?

How might you find out for sure? Do you know of a healthcare provider in your area who could test you?

What about Boosting Serotonin with Carbohydrates?

"Think of it as a Thanksgiving Day lived over and over again. Hygge is a movement, a feeling, and a state of mind that we need now more than ever, and eating our way toward togetherness seems like a pretty great way to start."

-Trine Hahnemann

Two of the hallmark symptoms of winter blues are an increased appetite & a craving for carbohydrates. It happens most likely, they say, because not getting enough sunlight leads to not having enough serotonin.

Enter carbohydrates. And often, weight gain.

And of course, we don't want that for ourselves this winter. But what do we do about food & cravings?

For me, the most important thing is to completely remove blame and/or shame. And resist the urge to navel-gaze about why I want to eat the cookies.

You *will* find something if you look. We probably all have wounds that haven't healed.

But this is about winter. And what you deserve is complete acceptance, compassion and kindness. And then, a meal plan.

Don't change everything without input from a healthcare provider you trust, but you might want to load your meal plan with foods that will make you feel better.

That's actually a good way to avoid overeating. Unless overeating is compulsive for you, and if it is, try working with someone who is an expert in that area to create an eating plan that helps you boost serotonin but doesn't endanger you emotionally.

I suggest adding something to every meal that will help boost serotonin and having a big cup of your favorite tea in between. Did you know that caffeine boosts serotonin?

We have all been warned away from carbohydrates but they *will* help you get back the serotonin you are missing during the winter. Talk to your dietitian about how to eat foods that will boost serotonin but not lead to weight gain.

Based on what I have read and experienced, if you create a plan that includes at least one carb at every meal (sweet potatoes, oatmeal, other whole grains), you are much less likely to dive into a carton of ice cream that night and emerge the winner. But I am not a dietitian or nutrition, so check with yours before making big changes.

And soup! Soup is a great good-for-you way to bring hygge warmth and comfort to winter along with a handy increase in serotonin.

Whether it's wild rice soup, loaded bakes potato soup, broccoli and cheese soup, or another favorite, a bowl of soup might be just the ticket this winter.

> *"Research has found that only small amounts of carbohydrate have to be eaten to make serotonin. Twenty-five to 30 grams of carbohydrate—the amount in one cup of Cheerios--is sufficient."* - Judith J. Wurtman, PhD

Personalizing this Section

Do you experience cravings for sweets and other carbohydrates during the winter?

If so, how do you manage them?

And were there any ideas suggested in this section that you think might help?

What might you try this winter?

How Might You Create Special Moments with the Ones You Love Most this Winter?

> *"What I've come to understand is that hygge is much more than simply a warm, cozy physical space. Hygge is, perhaps more importantly, a safe psychological space you enter into with your loved ones."* -Jessica Joelle Alexander, the co-author of The Danish Way of Parenting

That memory you have of your favorite family holiday celebration, or the way you feel when you think about being with your friends, that's hygge! The love and togetherness and sense of belonging and connection are all part of the hygge magic that you can tap into and create on purpose this winter.

I remember one winter, many years ago, a friend called me about half an hour before the movie started that she was inviting me to come see. Her friends had spontaneously decided to go see it and she wanted me to be there, too.

I was taking a nap when she called & it took a lot of convincing before I agreed to join them. I didn't feel like being sociable and was sure I wouldn't have a good time. But I did!

The movie is a blur, but then we went to a restaurant to get a bite to eat and as we talked about the movie and what it meant and what it might imply about our own lives, I loved that moment with them.

And I only knew my friend, so a group of strangers managed to include me enough to create a sense of safety & belonging, and I have never forgotten that night. That was a hygge moment.

Don't wait for holidays to create them. At least once a month, this winter, do something special that will create a moment of safety, of inclusion & belonging, of togetherness and make your winter warmer.

> *"Hygge moments are the small everyday moments that make you happy. The best of them are bright and shining like stars. Having a word for it makes you aware that they are right in front of your eyes. Ready for you to collect."* -Marie Tourell Soderberg, Hygge: The Danish Art of Happiness

Want some great ways to create hygge moments with family or friends all winter long?

Here they are…

Game Nights

Invite your friends and family over once a month or more for game nights.

Have everyone bring something, so all you need to do is have paper plates, bowls, etc., ready for them to use.

Suggest things that can be bought or are simple to make like potato chips and dip, cookies or other comfort food. Have warm beverages available, like tea or hot chocolate for anyone not interested in soda.

Instead of turning on fluorescent lighting above, have soft lighting everywhere, so the atmosphere is warm and cozy, but still well-lit.

Candles are a warm possibility as long as they are not right where the action is, so no one knocks them over while playing the games. Another idea is fairy lights here and there.

You could even do the game night weekly, if it takes off. And then, maybe leave the decorations up or pass them around so people can take turns hosting.

In my 20s, I was part of a group that got together every weekend, often more than once, and we had frequent game nights.

The ones I enjoyed most or remembered long afterward, were the ones where at least one of the games had fun & interesting "get to know you" kinds of questions. Where winning was about more than waiting to get to the end of the board or adding up which team answered the most questions correctly.

When was the last time you gathered a group of friends together for a game night?

It would be a great way to introduce friends to each other without the usual awkwardness because they both know you but don't know each other.

Movie Nights

Have a weekly or monthly movie night and whoever hosts gets to choose the movie, but doesn't have to supply the popcorn or the drinks. You could even have two: one family movie night each week and one movie night for friends each month.

Would it make winter more fun to plan for movie nights in advance and have them to look forward to each month?

Throw an Old-School-Music Dance Party During Whichever Month is Hardest for You

Think for a moment about the music you grew up with as a child or teen. Is there one favorite song or is it hard to narrow down?

Imagine in the boring dead of winter, getting a group of friends together, all about the same age, and asking each one to choose several "favorites" to share. You could even have everyone dress in an outfit that reflects the decade you have chosen.

Would it be fun to hang out all night, listening to them? Dancing to them?

Variation: do this with your family members.

I remember once, when I was about 9 or 10 years old, my mom ordered an album with 50s music on it.

It was the kind of thing you might see advertised at 3 o'clock in the morning, with snippets of each band performing the song just long enough to make you want to sing or dance to it. When it came, I could not wait to hear it, but my mother said we'd wait until after dinner, and I think that was the fastest meal I never tasted.

Finally, we were finished with dinner and my mom pushed back the couches and chairs and coffee table in the living room so we would have room to dance. She put the album on and we danced around the room from the first song to the last.

It was great fun! Would your family dance a bit if you put on a few oldies? Might be worth a try.

Throw a Comfort Food Pajama Party

> *"If you're looking to hygge (yes, it can be used as a verb), you'll want to light your fireplace, heat up some tea, pull on the wooliest socks you own, and throw together some comfort food. But not just any old comfort food. Hygge recipes should be totally decadent and warming, yet still pretty easy to make."*
>
> –13 Healthy Hygge Foods, Self magazine

I suggest making it a weekly event! But at least once a month, call your closest friends & invite them over for comfort food & sweet treats. You provide the sweet tea and hot chocolate and let them do the rest.

Pajamas means that when they go home, they can go right to bed & sleep off the carb coma.

I would call it serotonin night, for all the good feelings that togetherness + lighthearted fun + sweet comfort food will create. Light candles, have a fire going in the fireplace and let the light add a little cheer, too.

If you're an introvert like me, let me point out that these could be your two closest friends. Throwing a big party is more stress & pressure than it's worth when you prefer smaller gatherings or just a friend or two.

Variation: make it a family night, where you eat breakfast for dinner or let the kids stay up a little later to eat a sweet treat.

Would that be fun to do each week or once a month? Of course, your friends could share the hosting duties.

It could mean having something fun to look forward to each weekend. And each of these time-with-loved-ones ideas can be personalized and perfected so they work for you.

But the underlying concept is to give yourself some friend love and family love each week, to plan something you can look forward to and to create hygge moments that become lasting memories you can look back on fondly even before winter is over. If you can find a way to fill winter with fun moments, with hygge moments, you may win the mind game where winter blues is concerned.

Imagine looking forward to winter because you know you've got a lot of really fun things planned.

Personalizing this Section

What are the ideas mentioned here that could work for you?

Did reading them inspire any other ways you could make winter fun by spending hygge time with your loved ones?

Is there at least one idea you plan to try?

What's Your Hygge Happiness Superpower?

Part of the magic of choosing hygge strategies to help with winter blues is that you get to use the things you love most. And finding what those things are specifically for you is the most powerful magic of all.

Here's an exercise you can use to discover your hygge happiness superpower…

The Exercise

Take a few moments to think of at least ten happy memories from your past. Now, I don't mean milestone memories, like graduations or getting married or giving birth.

I mean simple, everyday moments of happiness where you felt like all was right with the world. Moments out of time that you wished wouldn't end.

Everyday moments of well-being, treasured in that moment. Jot down a word or two about each one to make sure you don't forget them because you're going to use them in the next exercise.

And once you've written them down, rate them according to which memory was best and then second-best, etc.

Mining for Gold

Once you have completed the exercise, let's take a closer look at the memories you chose, especially the ones with the highest ratings, and ask the following questions.

This is our second step in the process of finding your superpower.

When were you alone?

When were you with others?

What was the weather like?

Was there an activity?

Were you eating or drinking something?

Does anything else stand out to you about the memories or about any one of them, in particular?

Now, look at your top five memories. What do they have in common?

Noticing Connections

What do you notice about what your choices, or fave memories, have in common?

Specifically, look at your top five memories. What do they have in common? Does anything jump out at you?

How can you use this information to infuse your winter with happiness each day?

Make a commitment to doing so and then create your plan.

Personalizing this Section

If you had to write it out in a sentence, what would you say your hygge happiness superpower is?

How can you use this superpower every day, several times a day, when possible, during winter?

Create a sample schedule and try to include a hygge happiness moment in each segment of your day.

Making it Hygge & Happy

Your hygge happiness superpower will empower you more than you may yet realize. A happy day is just a series of happy moments.

A happy week is just a series of happy days. If you follow that concept, creating a happy winter may not be as impossible as it sometimes seems.

Especially if you are also using the other strategies this book offers.

For each hygge happiness moment, layer in as much hygge-ness as you can think of, so it's one for the memory books. Give that some thought as you take another look at the information you have gathered.

How Will You Use this Information to Transform Your Winter Experience?

My hope is that as you have been reading, you have gathered all the information you need to begin creating a highly personalized plan for tackling your winter blues symptoms and coming out on the other side completely victorious.

How do you feel as we come to the end? Are you more hopeful about what is possible this winter?

Do you feel more empowered than you did at the beginning of the book?

If you are thinking that you need more information, there is so much out there, and I encourage you to keep looking. I deliberately kept this book short so you wouldn't be overwhelmed by the time you got to the end of it.

And my hope was that you could read it while drinking a cup of tea, with paper and pen nearby so you could craft a plan in one afternoon.

I hope you have been able to do so and that you now know exactly what you will do to create your own happy winter.

Blessings to you!

Jeanine

The Happy Winter Guide Web Pages

I created several web pages that are connected to the book so that I could share with you some of the videos I found that you might want to see.

There are three pages, one for light therapy, one for exercise and one for comfort food. On the light therapy page, I share my own experiences with the light boxes I have tried.

They are password protected and you will need the password *hyggehealing*.

https://www.comfortwithhygge.com/lighttherapy.html

https://www.comfortwithhygge.com/comfortfoodideas.html

https://www.comfortwithhygge.com/exercise.html

Do You Know These 5 Facts About the Author?

She considers herself a cookie monster and has hardly ever met a cookie she didn't like.

She once won a karaoke contest singing Karen Carpenter's version of Superstar.

She once lost over 50 pounds without doing any exercise, so if you don't like exercise, she gets it!

She is old enough to have had winter blues before it had a name or an identity.

She made a wish for you that you, the one who is reading this right now, will create your own blissfully happy winter.

More about the Author

Jeanine Byers has loved writing since she was the editor of her school's newspaper in first grade. She read her first self-help book when she was 12 years old and she decided that someday she would write one, too.

She waited through college and grad school and training in several alternative healing modalities. She became a therapist, and then, a life coach, healer, spiritual director and homeschooling mom.

She created therapeutic programs, healing systems, healing techniques, and lots of homeschooling lesson plans.

Finally, she got tired of waiting to make her writing dream come true, and she has been writing happily ever since.

Printed in Great Britain
by Amazon